ROMAN

KEYCARD

BLACKWOOD

PRACTICE YOUR BIDDING

Master Point Press
331 Douglas Avenue
Toronto, Ontario, Canada
M5M 1H2

(416) 781-0351   Internet: **www.masterpointpress.com**

National Library of Canada Cataloguing in Publication

Seagram, Barbara
        Roman keycard Blackwood / Barbara Seagram & Linda Lee.

(Practice your bidding)
ISBN 1-894154-62-2

1. Contract bridge--Bidding. I. Lee, Linda (Linda Marcia), 1947- II. Title. III. Series.

GV1282.4.S4199 2003   795.41'52   C2003-902593-4

Design and layout: Olena S. Sullivan/New Mediatrix
Editor: Ray Lee

Printed and bound in Canada by Webcom Limited

1 2 3 4 5 6 7   09 08 07 06 05 04 03

ROMAN

KEYCARD

BLACKWOOD

Barbara Seagram & Linda Lee

MASTER POINT PRESS • TORONTO

PRACTICE YOUR BIDDING

The
PRACTICE YOUR BIDDING
Series

Jacoby 2NT

Roman Keycard Blackwood

Splinter Bids

Practice Your Slam Bidding (CD-ROM)

TABLE OF CONTENTS

HOW TO USE THIS BOOK

The purpose of this book is to help you and your partner practice Roman Keycard Blackwood and better understand how it is used. The book has been designed so it can be used either on your own or working with a partner. But while you will certainly get a lot out of it if you use it alone, it is especially good to use this book with your favorite partner to make sure that you are both on the same wavelength.

The first section of the book provides a refresher for the Roman Keycard Blackwood convention. Since cuebids are such an essential part of slam bidding we have also included a section on cuebidding. These parts of the book provide lots of examples but no exercises. Don't worry, you will get plenty of chance to practice in the rest of the book. For a more detailed explanation of Roman Keycard, and as a source of many other helpful conventions, you should refer to *25 Bridge Conventions You Should Know*, by Barbara Seagram and Marc Smith. Check the sections on Cuebids, Blackwood and Roman Keycard Blackwood to get the full story.

The last section of the book, 'Practice Hands', contains a set of forty pairs of North and South hands. You can cut them out or copy them and use them with a partner to practice bidding (don't try to do more than about ten at one sitting — that's more than enough to think and talk about at one time). We have provided space beside each hand to write down your auction; we suggest that you do this so you can refer to it when you are looking at the answers. You can also do this solo if you like: look at each hand in turn and write down the bid you would make at each step of the auction. Getting to the right spot is not the only goal; bidding the hand in the best way is another goal so, even if you see both hands, you will still need to work out the correct auction. When you have finished bidding the hands, look at the sample auctions and final contracts provided in the answer section. This book uses Standard American bidding in the sample auctions. There may be than one way to bid the hand, so don't worry if you don't duplicate our sequence exactly. Focus in particular on your use of Roman Keycard Blackwood and make sure that you get that right.

There is an earlier section of the book, entitled 'Working Alone' which contains the same practice deals. In this section, we show you just one of the hands and ask you a series of questions about how to bid it as the auction develops. Working through these exercises will teach you a lot more about the convention, so even if you go through the practice deals with a partner, we suggest you go through the questions and try to answer them. This will help you to make sure that you understand the convention thoroughly.

A final warning: don't expect to be perfect. Some of these hands are hard. So if you are doing better at the end of the book then at the beginning, you are doing very well indeed.

Since this is a book about Roman Keycard Blackwood you should expect that for almost all of the deals in the book, slam is a strong possibility. While this doesn't happen in real life, it will in this book, so enjoy it. But remember that, to keep you on your toes, not every hand will be suitable for Blackwood.

section
HOW ROMAN KEYCARD BLACKWOOD WORKS

What would slam bidding be without Blackwood? Blackwood is a convention designed to keep you from bidding slams that will fail because the partnership is missing two aces. Roman Keycard Blackwood serves exactly the same purpose but with added emphasis on honors in the trump suit. In Roman Keycard Blackwood, the king of trumps counts as an ace. This means that for the purposes of this convention, there are five aces in the deck!

Using Roman Keycard Blackwood

When you have decided that you want to go to slam if you have enough aces and good trumps, you bid Roman Keycard Blackwood. You have now 'taken charge of the auction'. You are asking questions and partner is answering those questions. You are the 'captain' of the auction and your partner is the 'crew'. This means that you are the one who is going to make the decision about the final contract. You ask the first question by bidding 4NT.

What is the Key Suit?

How do you know what the 'key suit' is — the suit in which you are going to count the king as an ace? Most of the time this will be easy — for example, if your side has clearly agreed on a trump suit — it has been bid and raised. If you have not specifically agreed on a trump suit, then the last suit bid is considered to be the trump suit. Here is a simple example of a key suit by inference.

Partner	You
1♡	4NT

Your 4NT bid is Roman Keycard Blackwood with hearts as trumps.

If your side has bid and raised two suits then the *first* suit that has been bid and raised is the key suit. Here is a more complex example auction:

Partner	You
1◇	1♡
2♡	3◇
3♠	4NT

Again, 4NT is Roman Keycard Blackwood with hearts as trumps.

Blackwood and Notrump Bidding

When partner opens the bidding with 1NT or 2NT, the process of asking for aces is different than over a one of a suit opening. This is because in notrump auctions you often need to use 4NT as a natural bid. For example, the auction

Partner	You
1NT	4NT

is a quantitative raise in notrump. This bid says to partner that you wish to play in no-trump and asks partner to bid 6NT with a maximum opener and pass with a minimum. So if you want to ask for aces directly over a notrump opening you should use the Gerber 4♣ convention. There is a description of the Gerber convention at the end of this section.

When is 4NT not Roman Keycard Blackwood in a notrump auction?
There are three situations you have to remember where 4NT is not Blackwood:

1. *Directly over an opening bid of 1NT or 2NT.*

Partner	You	Partner	You
1NT	4NT	2NT	4NT

In both these auctions, 4NT is not Roman Keycard Blackwood but a natural ('quantitative') raise of notrump (asking partner to go to 6NT with a maximum and pass with a minimum).

2. *Directly over a notrump rebid.*

Partner	You		Partner	You
1♡	1♠		1♣	1♡
2NT	4NT		1NT	4NT

Again, in these examples 4NT is a quantitative raise of notrump. It is not ace-asking

3. *After a notrump opening and a Stayman or Jacoby transfer.*

This one is a little more complicated so bear with us. Suppose that partner has opened 1NT and you have two questions to ask partner. First, do you want to play in a suit because I have a five-card major and second, do you have a maximum because I am interested in slam ?

For example you have:

♠ K Q 9 8 3 ♡ A 4 ◇ K 9 2 ♣ A 5 2

Here is how you ask both questions. First you let partner know about your five-card suit by transferring to your major. Here is the auction so far:

Partner	You
1NT	2♡
2♠	?

Now partner knows that you have five spades. The next step is to let partner know that you want him to go to slam with a maximum. To do that you rebid 4NT.

Partner	You
1NT	2♡
2♠	4NT
?	

So just as if you had bid 4NT directly, it is still not Blackwood, but a notrump raise: spades have not yet been agreed upon as trumps. The notrump opening bidder could have as few as two small spades for the 1NT opening bid. So, since a trump suit has not been agreed upon, 4NT is not Blackwood. However, partner knows about your spade suit now, so he can choose to play in 4NT, 5♠, 6♠ or 6NT.

This auction is similar:.

Partner	You
1NT	2♣
2♡	4NT

Again this is a notrump raise; if you like hearts and want to ask for aces here, use 4♣ (Gerber) instead.

4NT is always Roman Keycard Blackwood when a trump suit has been agreed. Once a trump suit has been agreed then 4NT is always Roman Keycard Blackwood, even if someone bids notrump naturally at some stage. Here are some examples.

Partner	You	Partner	You
1NT	4♡	1NT	2♡
4♠	4NT	2♠	3NT
		4♠	4NT

In the first case you have set spades as trumps with a 4♡ Texas transfer, (which shows a six-card spade suit) so 4NT is now Roman Keycard Blackwood with spades as the key suit. In the second example, partner has supported spades, so 4NT is Roman Keycard Blackwood despite your later 3NT bid.

Responses to Roman Keycard Blackwood

Since we now have five 'aces' or keycards to show, the responses are somewhat different from regular Blackwood. We suggest that you use the following system of responses — known as 1430.

- 5♣ 1 or 4 keycards
- 5◊ 3 or 0 keycards
- 5♡ 2 keycards without the queen of trumps
- 5♠ 2 keycards with the queen of trumps

The first two responses (1-4) and (3-0) form the number 1430. This happens to be the score for a small slam in a major at duplicate bridge so it makes it an easy number to remember.

Some people play a variation of this where they invert the first two responses (playing 03-14). This method works just as well as 1430, so if you are playing with a new partner it is wise to check which way they would like to play. This is not something you want to get mixed up!

How can you tell exactly how many keycards partner has?

You will notice that the first two responses, 5♣ and 5♢, are some-what ambiguous. With 5♣ partner could have one keycard or four and with 5♢ partner could have zero keycards or three. How can you tell the difference? Most of the time, it will be perfectly clear from your hand and the rest of the auction. Let us say that you have

♠ 6 ♡ K Q J 8 5 2 ♢ K Q 10 9 ♣ A Q

Partner	You
1♣	1♡
3♡	4NT
5♢	

Partner is showing three or zero keycards. Can you tell which? Of course partner must have three keycards. Partner has shown a min-imum of 16 points. There are only 11 high cards missing outside of the three aces. Partner could not have enough for a three heart bid without any aces. Similarly, if partner had bid 5♣, showing one or four keycards, we would know that he had just one — we have two keycards and there are only three left. (There are only five keycards, never six.)

When to use Blackwood

The Blackwood convention is intended to be used when you have decided to play in slam, as long as your side is not missing too many aces. Blackwood is not meant as a way to get you to slam, it is a con-vention designed to stop you from getting to a bad slam.

Let us say that you have decided that your side has the values (i.e. points and shape) to make slam. Your only concern is that the opponents may be able to cash too many aces. Is now the time to bid Blackwood? Yes but... you still have to pass a few more hur-dles.

When not to use the Blackwood Convention

1) *You should not bid Blackwood with an unprotected side suit — one where you don't have first- or second-round control.* The main danger is that you will not be able to tell whether you should go on to slam if even if you are only missing one keycard. If you have an unprotected suit, partner may have

enough keycards and slam may still fail, because the opponents can take the ace and king in this unprotected suit before you can even discard anything. Let us look at a case like that. You have

♠ 4 3   ♡ A K 10 5 4   ◊ A 4   ♣ K Q 4 2

Here is the auction:

Partner	You
1◊	1♡
3♡	?

How do you like your slam chances? Slam looks very good. You have 16 HCP and partner has shown 16-18 points in support of hearts. Only one problem — what if your side has two quick spade losers? Partner's hand might be one of these:

1) ♠ Q 5   ♡ Q J 10 8   ◊ K Q J 9 8   ♣ A J
2) ♠ A J   ♡ Q J 10 8   ◊ K Q J 9 8   ♣ J 5
3) ♠ K Q   ♡ Q 10 8 5   ◊ K Q 9 8 7   ♣ A 5

If he has the first hand the opponents can defeat the slam by cashing the first two spades. If he has the second or third hand, slam will make. However, Roman Keycard Blackwood won't help, as in all cases partner will show one keycard. The difference is that in the last two hands partner is able to provide control of the spade suit. Using Blackwood is not appropriate until you know that spades are controlled. We will show you what to do instead of using Blackwood with hands like this.

2) *You should not use Roman Keycard Blackwood when you have a void.* You really don't care about the ace in your void suit but partner doesn't know that. If you are missing two keycards, one of them may be in your void suit and so you might have enough for slam anyway — but Blackwood won't tell you that.

As an example, your hand is

♠ —   ♡ A 10 7 4 3   ◊ K Q J 10 3 2   ♣ K 2

Partner	You
1♣	1◊
1♡	?

After partner surprises you with his 1♡ rebid you are pretty certain you want to be in slam. You want to make certain that your side is not missing too many keycards. Normally Roman Keycard Blackwood would be just the ticket, but not with your spade void. If partner does not show all the keycards you cannot be certain whether partner has the right stuff. Partner could have any of these hands:

1) ♠ A Q 2 ♡ Q 8 6 2 ◊ 7 ♣ A Q 5 4 2
2) ♠ Q 5 4 ♡ K Q 7 6 ◊ 8 ♣ A Q 5 4 2
3) ♠ J 9 ♡ K Q 7 6 ◊ A 8 ♣ A Q 5 4 2
4) ♠ A 9 ♡ K Q 7 6 ◊ 8 5 ♣ A Q 5 4 2

With the first hand you cannot make a slam, but with the second you can make 6♡ comfortably. Partner will respond the same 5♠ to Roman Keycard Blackwood with either hand. Partner will also make the same response (5◊) on both hand three and hand four but you can make a grand slam opposite hand three, while six hearts is the limit if he has hand four. Roman Keycard Blackwood just doesn't work well on hands with voids. The method of dealing with these hands is similar to when you have two or three small cards in a side suit. We will come back to this.

Locating the Queen of Trumps

The queen of trumps is often a very important card when you are considering bidding a slam. For example, if your side has all the keycards you may need to find out about the queen of trumps before you decide to commit to the seven-level. If partner's response has shown two keycards, he will already have provided this information, since 5♡ shows two keycards without the queen and 5♠ shows two keycards with it. But what if partner has responded with 5♣ or 5◊? There is still a way to find out. You make the cheapest possible five-level bid, other than the trump suit, to ask partner this question.

Look at these examples:

Partner	You
1◊	1♡
3♡	4NT
5♣	5◊

The cheapest bid, 5◊, asks partner about the ♡Q.

Partner	You
1♢	1♡
3♡	4NT
5♢	5♠

Here 5♡ is the cheapest bid but we skip the trump suit and bid 5♠ to ask for the trump queen. (This is because 5♡ would be a signoff in hearts.)

Partner responds to the Queen-ask as follows:

Trump suit at lowest level (usually five-level)	No trump queen
Jump to six of the trump suit	Queen of trumps and no side kings
Other suit	Queen of trumps and a king in the suit you bid. Do not bid higher than six of the trump suit. If showing your cheapest side king would take you too high, then bid 5NT.
5NT	Queen of trumps and a king in a suit that is higher-ranking than the trump suit.

Here are two example auctions

West	East
1♡	3♡
4NT	5♣ [1]
5♢ [2]	5♠ [3]

1. 1 or 4 keycards
2. Queen-ask
3. Heart queen and spade king

West	East
1♢	3♢ [1]
4NT	5♣ [2]
5♡ [3]	5NT [4]

1. Limit raise
2. 1 or 4 keycards
3. Queen-ask (could not bid 5♢ as partner would now pass, so we have to skip this level)
4. Diamond queen and king of hearts

Note that we can determine in the last example that the side king must be the heart king. The other two side kings could have been shown below 6♢.

Looking for kings

If your side has all the keycards, you may want to find out about partner's kings instead of inquiring about the trump queen. You may know the location of the trump queen (for example, if you have it yourself). In this case you continue with 5NT and partner tells you how many side kings he has, using the same responses as in regular Blackwood:

Note that now the king of trumps is *not* included in this interrogation as we have already discovered its presence or absence via the response to the 4NT question.

6♣ no side kings
6◇ one side king
6♡ two side kings
6♠ three side kings

However, remember that there are only three side kings in total. Here is an example.

♠ K 2 ♡ A Q J 9 8 ◇ A Q J 10 ♣ K 2

Partner	You
1♣	2♡
3♡	4NT
5◇	5NT
6◇	7NT

Partner opens the bidding and you have nineteen high card points — slam territory. Once you have found the heart fit you jump to Roman Keycard Blackwood. Partner bids 5◇ showing zero or three. If partner does not have three keycards, he can only have nine high card points so you know partner must have three. Your side has all the keycards. What do you need for the grand slam? The ◇K. When you ask for kings, partner bids 6◇ which shows one of the three available (he has already shown the trump king). This can only be the ◇K. Your side has at least thirteen tricks so you bid the grand slam. Partner's hand?

♠ A 5 4 ♡ K 6 5 2 ◇ K 2 ♣ A 10 4 3

A Review of Cuebids

A cuebid is a bid made to show a first- or second-round control in a suit. Having a 'control' means that you can stop the opponents from taking too many winners in that suit by winning the trick yourself. Here are examples of controls in the spade suit when hearts are trumps:

- a) ♠ A 3 2
- b) ♠ —
- c) ♠ K 5
- d) ♠ 6

Examples (a) and (b) show first-round spade control: if spades are led you will be able to take the first trick. In example (a) you will win the ace and in example (b) you will trump the spade. Examples (c) and (d) show a second-round control in spades: if the opponents lead spades you will be able to take the second trick. Note that there is some risk with example (c) if the spade is led through the ♠K (assuming partner does not have the ♠Q), but this still counts as a control.

Sometimes we use cuebids on our way to slam. We will use them both to indicate slam interest and to show partner that we have a control in a suit.

In order to make a slam, your side must have controls in all of the side suits. Here is an example of a hand with many tricks but where you can't make slam:

West	East
♠ A J 5 4 3	♠ K Q 10 9 7
♡ 5 4	♡ 9 2
◇ K Q J 10 9	◇ A
♣ A	♣ K Q J 10 9

These hands have fifteen top tricks. Unfortunately the opponents have the first two tricks in hearts so slam cannot be made! East–West do not have a heart control.

When is a bid a cuebid?

How do you know if a bid of a new suit is a cuebid? A new suit bid is only a control if our side has agreed on a trump suit and committed to play at least in game. Lets look at each of these components in turn.

West	East	West	East
1♠	2♦	1♡	4♡
3♣		4♠	

In the first auction 3♣ is not a cuebid — it shows clubs. We have not agreed on a trump suit.

In the second auction, 4♠ is a cuebid. We have already agreed that hearts are trumps.

Even if we have agreed on a trump suit, a new suit is not a cuebid if we have not yet committed to play in game. If we can sign off below game, then the new suit is just a game try giving us a choice of game or partscore contracts.

Auction 1		Auction 2		Auction 3		Auction 4	
West	East	West	East	West	East	West	East
1♠	2♠	1♦	1♡	1♡	2♦	1♠	3♠
3♦		2♡	3♣	3♦	3♠	4♣	

In the first two auctions we have agreed on the trump suit but we have not committed to playing the hand in game. In each case the new suit bid is a game try. The third auction is a bit more complicated. Here 3♠ is a bid showing a notrump stopper and suggesting game in notrump. It is a kind of game try but is suggesting the possibility of game in notrump as well as game in diamonds. If the West hand is not suitable for notrump, West can still sign off in a partscore of 4♦. This kind of two-way bid is common when the trump suit is a minor. In the last auction, 4♣ is a cuebid. Once you bid at the four-level your side is committed to the spade game, so it makes no sense for 4♣ to be a game try. It must be a slam try. It shows first-round control of clubs.

What suit should you cuebid?

What suit should you cuebid? You start by bidding first-round controls first, and you bid your cheapest first round control first. 'Cheapest' means that you bid the next one up the line in the auction. The advantage of this is that when you bypass a side suit you deny having the first-round control in that suit. Later, you bid your second-round controls as cheaply as possible.

Note that we never cuebid first- or second-round control in the trump suit.

Here are some examples:

West	East
1♡	3♡
?	

In this auction spades is the 'cheapest' cuebid, clubs second and diamonds last.

As West you hold:

A) ♠ 5 4 ♡ A Q J 4 3 2 ◇ A K J ♣ A 2
B) ♠ 5 4 ♡ A K 10 4 3 2 ◇ A 2 ♣ K Q J
C) ♠ A 2 ♡ A K J 7 4 3 ◇ 5 4 ♣ K Q J

Hand A) bid 4♣. This shows a first-round club control and denies a first-round spade control.

Hand B) bid 4◇. This shows a first-round diamond control and denies a first-round control in clubs or spades.

Hand C) bid 3♠. This shows a first-round spade control. Here is an example of a hand where we use cuebidding to get to a slam:

Partner	You
♠ A 7	♠ 3 2
♡ K J 5 4	♡ A Q 10 9 3 2
◇ 8 7	◇ A K Q 5
♣ K Q J 10 3	♣ 2
1♣	1♡
3♡	4◇ [1]
4♠ [1]	4NT [2]
5♡	6♡

1. Cuebid
2. RKC Blackwood

When partner double raises hearts, you suspect that there may be a slam since you have a very nice hand. However you need some controls in the black suits, especially in spades. (You must not use Blackwood immediately because you have two small spades.) When you cuebid 4◇, you alert partner about your slam interest. You also show partner the first-round diamond control but deny first-round controls in spades and clubs. With good controls in the black suits, partner shows you his spade control. It is now safe to bid Roman Keycard Blackwood. Partner shows you two keycards, and you now can safely bid 6♡.

This may seem very complicated but even using the occasional cuebid combined with Roman Keycard Blackwood will make your slam bidding much more accurate.

A Review of Gerber

Gerber is a convention used to ask for aces and kings when you plan to play the hand in notrump. There is no need to worry about a key suit or key cards because you are planning to play the hand in notrump. Note that 4♣ is only Gerber when the last bid was a real notrump bid (i.e. it shows a very specific point count).

The Gerber convention is a lot like Blackwood. When you use it, you become the captain of the auction and ask partner a question. Partner responds to your question, and you decide where to play the hand. Gerber asks partner how many aces he has. It starts with the bid of 4♣. Parter responds as follows:

4♦	zero or four aces
4♥	one ace
4♠	two aces
4NT	three aces

What do you do if you do not have enough aces for slam?

You end the auction by bidding the minimum level of notrump (normally 4NT). For example:

Partner	You
2NT	4♣
4♠	4NT

The 4NT bid cannot be asking for aces. You already did that with 4♣. It is to play.

After partner responds to 4♣, you can ask for kings in much the same way by bidding 5♣. The responses are the same only this time partner tells you how many kings you have instead of how many aces, responding at the five-level.

5♦	zero or four kings
5♥	one king
5♠	two kings
5NT	three kings

Here is an example of a Gerber auction:

Partner	You
1NT	4♣[1]
4♡[2]	5♣[3]
5♠[4]	6NT

1. Gerber
2. 1 ace
3. Asking for kings
4. 2 kings

WORKING ALONE (QUESTIONS)

Deal 1

SOUTH
♠ 6 3
♡ K J 10 3 2
◇ A 9 5
♣ K Q 2

The auction starts:

North	South
	1♡
3♣	4♣
4NT	

1. 4NT is Roman Keycard Blackwood. What is the key suit?
2. What is your correct response and what does it show?
3. If partner continues with 5NT what is he asking and what is the correct response?

Deal 2

NORTH
♠ K Q J 10 3 2
♡ K Q 9
◇ A 2
♣ K J

The auction starts:

North	South
1♠	3♠[1]

1. Limit raise

1. What should you do now?
2. If you use Roman Keycard Blackwood, what does each of the following responses indicate and what action should you take?
   a) 5♣   b) 5♡

Deal 3

SOUTH
♠ 6
♡ K J 9 4 3
◊ A 9 8 2
♣ A J 3

1. If hearts have been agreed as the trump suit, what is your correct response to Roman Keycard Blackwood?
2. When you respond showing keycards with hearts as trumps, how does partner ask for the queen of trumps?
3. If partner asks for kings with 5NT, how do you respond?

Deal 4

NORTH
♠ A Q 10 9 8 7 6
♡ 3
◊ A Q 5 4
♣ 2

1. Partner has opened 1NT; how do you like your slam chances? What do you need to know to decide if you should play in slam?
2. How can you find out about partner's keycards?
3. If partner shows two keycards, where would you like to play this hand?

Deal 5

NORTH
♠ A Q J 8 4 3 2
♡ 2
◊ 5
♣ A K Q 8

1. You open this hand 1♠ and partner bids 2NT (Jacoby, showing a forcing raise in spades). You know partner has four spades and at least an opening bid. What do you need to make slam? Is there any way you can find out the information you need?
2. If you bid Roman Keycard Blackwood and partner showed two keycards, what would you do?
3. What if partner showed three keycards?

Deal 6

NORTH
♠ A J 5
♡ A Q 8 2
◊ K 2
♣ Q J 10 9

1. You open this hand 1NT and partner transfers to spades and then bids hearts. This shows at least five spades and at least five hearts and a hand that can force to game. You have a great fit with both of partner's suits. What suit should you support?
2. If partner bids 4NT now, what does this mean?
3. If it is Keycard Blackwood, what is the key suit?
4. How do you respond to Roman Keycard Blackwood?

Deal 7

SOUTH

♠ K Q 10 7 6
♡ A J 9 2
♢ 9 8
♣ A K

1. You open this hand 1♠ and partner makes a splinter bid with a bid of 4♢. This shows a diamond singleton or void and enough support points to make a spade game. What should you do now?

2. If you bid Roman Keycard Blackwood on this hand, what do the following responses by partner indicate to you?
   a) 5♣
   b) 5♢

3. What would you do next over partner's response of
   a) 5♣?
   b) 5♢?

Deal 8

SOUTH

♠ J 9 3
♡ A
♢ A Q 5 4
♣ A K 9 8 5

1. Your partner has opened this hand with a bid of 2♠ (weak). How do you like your chances for a spade game? A spade slam?

2. You bid 2NT (asking partner to show a feature) over partner's 2♠ bid. Which of the following rebids from partner makes your hand better and which makes it worse?
   a) 3♢
   b) 3♡

3. If you bid 4NT and partner responds 5♣, should you ask for the spade queen? Why or why not?

Deal 9

NORTH

♠ K Q
♡ A Q J
♢ A Q J 10 8 7 5
♣ A

1. For once you have a hand you deserve. When you open this hand with 2♣, your partner makes a waiting bid of 2♢. What should you bid now?

2. Your partner raises your diamond bid. What do you need to make slam?

3. If you bid Roman Keycard Blackwood after your partner has supported diamonds, what do you do after each of the following responses?
   a) 5♣   b) 5♢   c) 5♡

Deal 10

SOUTH
♠ K 10 4 3 2
♡ J 6 3
◇ K 9
♣ A K 2

1. What should you open this hand and why?
2. If you open 1♠ and partner responds 2♡, what should you do now?
3. Hearts are agreed as trumps. How do you respond to 4NT?
4. Partner continues with 5NT. What should you bid now and why?

Deal 11

SOUTH
♠ Q 10 9
♡ A 9 8
◇ K Q 3
♣ A Q 6 4

1. Partner opens 1NT. Do you think slam is a possibility? Do you expect to play in a suit or notrump?
2. If you decide to ask for aces, what would you bid now?

Deal 12

NORTH
♠ K 8 4 3
♡ A J 4 3
◇ A J 3
♣ K 9 8

1. Partner opens 1♠ and you bid Jacoby 2NT showing a game raise in spades with at least four-card trump support. Partner rebids 4◇, showing a good five-card diamond suit. Has this bid improved your hand?
2. Suppose the auction has proceeded this way:

North	South
	1♠
2NT	4◇
4NT	5♣

What does partner's 5♣ bid show, and what should you do now?

Deal 13

NORTH
♠ K 9 8 7 3
♡ 9
◇ A K 6 5 4 3
♣ A

The auction starts

North	South
1◇	1♡
1♠	2♣
?	

1. 2♣ is 'fourth-suit forcing'. By the way, fourth-suit forcing is a special convention which is used

to set up a game force but does not necessarily show clubs. (For more information about fourth suit forcing refer to *25 Conventions You Should Know*). Now that you know that partner has at least an opening bid, are you ready to bid Roman Keycard Blackwood?

2. Partner agrees diamonds as the trump suit. Later he bids 4NT (Roman Keycard Blackwood); what is your correct response?

3. How would partner check for the ◇Q and why would he want to?

4. If partner asks for the ◇Q, what would you respond?

Deal 14

SOUTH
♠ A K 5 4
♡ Q 5 3
◇ A K Q 3
♣ A 2

1. Partner starts off with a preempt of 3♡ showing a seven-card heart suit. Where do you think you might end up on this hand?

2. If you bid 4NT (Roman Keycard Blackwood), partner responds 5♣. Are you going to play this hand in slam?

Deal 15

NORTH
♠ Q 9 8
♡ A Q J 4 2
◇ K 6
♣ A 5 3

1. Partner opens 1♠. What should you respond?

2. Suppose the auction continues like this:

North	South
	1♠
2♡	3♠
?	

Partner's bids shows a good six-card spade suit and 16-18 points. You decide that you want to be in a spade slam if you are not off too many keycards. If you bid 4NT now will partner know that spades are the key suit?

3. If partner bids 5◇ can you tell for sure exactly how many keycards partner has?

Deal 16

NORTH
♠ 5
♡ A Q J 10 9 5 4
◇ K Q J 9 5
♣ —

1. You open 1♡ and partner responds 1♠. What should you bid now and why?
2. Here is the auction to date

North	South
1♡	1♠
3◇	3♡
?	

   a) What does partner's 3♡ bid mean?
   b) Do you think that you have slam chances?
   c) What should you do now?

Deal 17

SOUTH
♠ K Q 9 8
♡ K 6 5 4
◇ Q 10
♣ A J 7

You open this hand with 1NT. The auction continues as follows:

North	South
	1NT
2◇ 1	2♡
3◇	?

1. Transfer to hearts

1. Partner's bids show a hand with at least five hearts and at least four diamonds and values which are enough for game opposite your 1NT opening. He is asking you to support hearts or diamonds or even play in notrump. What should you do now?
2. After hearts are agreed as trumps, partner bids Roman Keycard Blackwood. What is your response?
3. If partner continues by asking for kings with 5NT, what do you respond now?

Deal 18

SOUTH

♠ A K Q 8 7 6
♡ 3
◇ A 7 2
♣ 5 4

1. The auction has proceeded

North	South
	1♠
2♡	3♠
4NT	

a) What is the key suit?
b) What is the correct response?
c) How does partner ask for the queen of trumps now?

Deal 19

SOUTH

♠ K 9 8
♡ A 4 3
◇ K 3
♣ A 10 9 8 7

1. Partner opens the bidding with 1♠. What is your correct response?
2. What would you do if partner now rebid 2♠?
3. What would you do if partner rebid 3♠?

Deal 20

NORTH

♠ 3
♡ J 10 8 7
◇ A K Q J 9 8
♣ A 2

This has been the auction so far.

North	South
	1♡
2NT	3♡
4NT	5◇

1. What does partner's 5◇ bid show?
2. How do you ask for the trump queen?
3. If partner responds 6♣ to your queen-ask, what do you do?

Deal 21

SOUTH

♠ 9 8 7 6
♡ A 9 8
◇ A 5
♣ K Q 9 5

1. After spades have been bid and raised, partner bids Roman Keycard Blackwood. What is your response?
2. If partner then bids 5NT to ask for kings, what is your response?

Deal 22

NORTH
♠ K 8 4
♡ A Q
◇ K Q 10
♣ K 9 8 7 5

1. Partner opens the bidding 1NT. Should you use Roman Keycard Blackwood now?
2. What will you do if partner shows two aces?
3. What bid from partner will show two aces?

Deal 23

NORTH
♠ 5
♡ 5
◇ A K Q 9 8 7
♣ K Q J 10 9

The auction has started:

North	South
	1♡
2◇	3◇
?	

1. Hurray for partner, for once he has trump support when we have a distributional hand. What should you bid now?
2. If you bid Roman Keycard Blackwood, will you be at risk if partner does not have enough keycards?

Deal 24

NORTH
♠ —
♡ K Q 10 9 7
◇ Q J 7 3 2
♣ Q 9 5

1. If hearts are agreed as trumps, and partner bids Roman Keycard Blackwood, what is your correct response?
2. Assume the auction has proceeded as follows:

North	South
1♡	2♣
2◇	4NT
5◇	5♡
?	

What does the 5♡ bid mean, and what is your correct response?

Deal 25

NORTH
♠ K Q 10 9 6 2
♡ 9
♢ K 7
♣ A J 8 5

1. What would you bid if partner opened 1NT? (This will require two answers — your first response and your next bid after partner rebids.)
2. What does the following auction mean?

North	South
	2NT
3♡	3♠
4NT	

Deal 26

NORTH
♠ K
♡ A Q 8 6 3
♢ A 10 6
♣ A Q J 10

1. You open 1♡ and your partner splinters in diamonds. What are you looking for to make slam?
2. The auction has proceeded

North	South
1♡	4♢
4NT	5♡
5NT	6♢
?	

What does partner's 6♢ bid mean, and what should you do next?

Deal 27

NORTH
♠ A Q 10 9 8 6
♡ A Q 8
♢ A 7
♣ K 2

1. Partner opens 1♡. What should you bid now?
2. If you decide to bid 1♠ and partner rebids 2♡, how do you like your slam chances?
3. If you bid Roman Keycard for hearts and partner shows two keycards, what would you do next?

Deal 28

NORTH
♠ 8
♡ A 10 5
♢ A K J 10 8 7
♣ A J 2

1. You open the bidding 1♢. What do you expect to rebid?
2. During the auction partner raises diamonds and later uses Roman Keycard Blackwood. What is your response? If you had already cuebid hearts, does this change anything?

Deal 29

SOUTH
♠ 3
♡ A Q 10 9 3
◇ K 9 8
♣ A K Q J

1. Partner opens 1♡ and shows a singleton club when you force to game in hearts with Jacoby 2NT. You know that you have a lot of high cards in clubs opposite partner's singleton. Should you try for slam anyway?
2. Partner has opened 1♡. With hearts agreed as trumps, you bid Roman Keycard Blackwood. If partner responds 5♣, how many keycards does he have? What if he responds 5◇?

Deal 30

SOUTH
♠ A Q J 10 5
♡ A K Q 7 5
◇ —
♣ K Q 7

1. What do you open this great hand? What is your plan for the auction?
2. After partner supports spades, there are only two cards you need for a grand slam. Is it time to bid Roman Keycard Blackwood to find out about them?
3. Once partner supports spades, how do you proceed?

Deal 31

SOUTH
♠ A K
♡ AKQJ10875
◇ 9
♣ A 10

1. Wow, this is one of the best hands we have ever seen. What do you need to make a small slam? What do you need to make a grand slam?
2. Partner has shown some values. After establishing hearts as trumps, you bid Roman Keycard Blackwood. If partner showed one keycard, what would you do?

Deal 32

NORTH
♠ K 9 3
♡ A K 8 3 2
◇ K Q 9
♣ A 5

1. You open with 1♡ and partner bids 4♡ (preemptive). What should you do now?
2. Partner bids 4NT Roman Keycard Blackwood over your 1♡ bid. What is the key suit and what should your respond?

Deal 33

SOUTH
♠ Q 9 5 4
♡ A Q 8
◇ A 7
♣ A 5 3 2

The auction has started:

North	South
1♣	1♠
4♠	?

1 a) What does partner's 4♠ bid mean?
   b) Should you use Roman Keycard Blackwood now?
2. If you use Roman Keycard Blackwood and partner responds 5♡, what will you do now?

Deal 34

SOUTH
♠ A K 3
♡ K Q J 8 5
◇ 9
♣ A 5 4 2

1. You open this hand with 1♡ and partner bids 2♣. What should you rebid and why?
2. With clubs as trumps, should you bid Roman Keycard Blackwood if partner expresses some slam interest?

Deal 35

SOUTH
♠ K Q J 10 7
♡ 5
◇ K 10
♣ A K J 9 8

1. Partner opens 1NT. What is your plan for bidding this hand?
2. The auction has gone as follows:

North	South
1NT	2♡
2♠	3♣
3♠	?

a) What does 3♠ mean?
b) Is a 4NT bid now Roman Keycard Blackwood or a notrump raise?

Deal 36

NORTH

♠ Q 10 9 8 2
♡ A 5 4
◇ K 10
♣ A J 3

1. Partner has opened 1◇ and you bid 1♠. What would you do now if partner bid a) 4♠? c) 4♣ ?
2. The auction proceeds as follows:

North	South
	1◇
1♠	4♠
4NT	5♣

What does partner's 5♣ bid show? What would you do next?

Deal 37

NORTH

♠ A 4
♡ 7 5 4 2
◇ K Q J 7 5
♣ K 2

1. Hearts are trumps and partner has shown a very strong hand (more than twenty points) with at least five hearts. You bid Roman Keycard Blackwood with hearts as the key suit. How would you continue if partner bid
   a) 5♣?   b) 5◇?
2. Assume that your partner has bid 5♣ over your 4NT, and you ask partner for the ♡Q. What does it mean if he bids 6♡? What about 5NT?

Deal 38

SOUTH

♠ K Q
♡ J 10
◇ A K Q 10 3
♣ K Q 5 3

1. What would you respond if partner opened 1♡?
2. You bid diamonds over partner's 1♡ opening, and partner rebids hearts. If you now jump to 4NT, what is the key suit?

Deal 39

SOUTH

♠ K 10 7 6 5
♡ A 6
◇ A J 8 6
♣ K J

1. You open this hand 1♠ and partner bids 3♠ (limit raise). What should you do now?
2. What if partner bid 4NT over your one spade bid. Is this Roman Keycard Blackwood. If so what is the key suit? What would you respond?

Deal 40

NORTH

♠ 7 6
♡ 9
◇ K Q 10 9 6 5 4
♣ 9 8 4

1. You open the auction with a preemptive 3◇ and partner bids 4NT. Is that Roman Keycard Blackwood?
2. What do you bid now?

WORKING ALONE (answers)

Deal 1

1. Clubs is the key suit. Clubs were bid by partner and raised by you.
2. Bid 5♠. This shows two keycards, (you have the ◇A and the ♣K) and also shows the queen of trumps, the ♣Q.
3. Partner is asking about your kings. Bid 6◇. You have exactly one king (not counting the ♣K which you have already shown).

Deal 2

1. Bid 4NT. You have 19 HCP and a six-card suit. When partner shows a fit and a limit raise you are in the slam zone. Your only problem is that you are missing three aces. If partner has at least two of them you have excellent slam chances.
2. a) 5♣ shows one or four keycards. There are only three keycards missing, so you know partner has exactly one. Bid 5♠; you are missing two aces.
3. b) 5♡ shows two keycards without the ♠Q. You are only missing one keycard. This should be enough for slam. Bid 6♠.

Deal 3

1. Bid 5◇. This shows three keycards.
2. Partner bids 5♠ to ask for the queen of trumps over your 5◇ bid. Partner makes the cheapest bid excluding trumps.
3. You respond 6♣ showing zero kings. You have already shown the ♡K.

Deal 4

1. Slam chances look excellent. You would like to find out if partner has enough keycards to make slam. The ◊K is also a useful card.

2. If you just bid 4NT now it is not Blackwood. It is 'quantitative' — a request for partner to go to 6NT with a maximum. Your first step is to establish spades as trumps, and you do this by transferring to spades. If you play Texas transfers, transfer to spades at the four-level, indicating that you do not want to play in notrump. Now spades is the trump suit and partner knows that a subsequent 4NT bid is Roman Keycard Blackwood in spades. If you don't play transfers, you should start with a forcing jump to 3♠.

3. Two keycards are enough for slam. It is possible that slam may not be cold if partner does not have the ◊K, but 6♠ should have a good play opposite any hand partner has.

Deal 5

1. Bid 4NT — Roman Keycard Blackwood; it will tell you what you need to know. This hand will make slam if partner has enough keycards. Your hand has only three losers, the ♠K and the two red aces. There is no need to tell partner more about your hand or find out any more about partners hand

2. Bid 6♠. You are missing one keycard.

3. Bid 7♠. Your nice partner has filled in all your losers. You can make a grand slam.

Deal 6

1. Support hearts. You have four hearts and only three spades. You would be happy to play in either suit but given the choice you like hearts better.

2. This is Roman Keycard Blackwood. Hearts have been bid and raised so hearts is the key suit.

3. Bid 5♠. This shows two keycards and the ♡Q.

Deal 7

1. Bid 4NT. When partner shows diamond shortness your hand has improved. Partner has zero high cards in diamonds so he has to have a lot of goodies in the majors. If your side has enough

controls slam should be there. For example, partner might have:
♠ A 9 8 3 ♡ K 5 4 ◇ 5 ♣ Q J 7 5 2.

2. a) Partner is showing one keycard. You have three of the five keycards; partner cannot have four.

 b) Partner is showing zero keycards. Partner can't have three because you have three of the five.

 c) Partner is showing two keycards without the ♠Q. You are not surprised about the latter since you have it. Your side has all the keycards.

3 a) Bid 6♠. You have enough keycards for a small slam.

 b) Bid 5♠. You are short two keycards.

Deal 8

1. Game is certain and slam is a possibility.

2. a) The 3◇ bid makes your hand better because partner is showing the ◇K which will fill in your diamond suit. You will make twelve tricks if partner's spades are good — one heart, five minor-suit tricks, at least five spades in partner's hand and a heart ruff in your hand.

 b) A 3♡ rebid makes your hand worse because partner has a wasted heart honor. Slam is less likely.

3. Bid 6♠ if you play weak two-bids as recommended in *25 Conventions You Should Know*. Partner should have two of the top three honors, or one of the top two and three of the top five. You know that partner is missing one of the top two from his response to Roman Keycard Blackwood. You have the ♠J so partner must have the ♠Q and ♠10. However, you could ask for the queen just to be sure.

Deal 9

1. Bid 3◇. You could rebid notrump but this hand is unbalanced and will probably play better in a suit.

2. You have three possible losers — the ♠A, ◇K and ♡K. Partner will have to take care of at least two of them.

3. a) Bid 6◇. Partner is showing one keycard. This is enough to give you a reasonable chance for slam.

 b) Pass. Partner has no keycards.

c) Bid 5 NT. Partner has both of the missing keycards. If partner has an additional king bid 7◇, as the grand slam is likely to be cold. If partner has the ♡K you have thirteen tricks. If partner has the ♣K and not the K ♡ you still have thirteen tricks (unless partner has only two spades). You have three spade tricks, one heart trick, seven diamonds and two clubs.

Deal 10

1. Bid 1♠. This hand is balanced but you do not have enough high cards to open 1NT.
2. Bid 3♡. You have support for partner. Let him know. Remember that responder must have 5 cards in ♡ suit for his response of 2 ♡.
3. Bid 5♣. This shows one keycard, (the ♣A).
4. Bid 6♠. This shows all three of your kings outside the trump suit.

Deal 11

1. Yes, slam is likely. You have enough points for a slam opposite partner's 15-17 HCP. Since both you and partner have balanced hands you plan to play this hand in notrump, and you want to ask partner for aces.
2. Bid 4♣, Gerber. Note that 4NT is not Blackwood since you have not agreed on a trump suit. A bid of 4NT here is a quantitative notrump raise, asking partner to bid 6 NT with a maximum.

Deal 12

1. Partner's 4◇ bid does improve your hand. If partner has a good five-card diamond suit, your diamond cards will act as fillers for partner and that suit will provide a lot of tricks.
2. The 5♣ response shows that partner has one keycard, so you are missing one keycard. Bid 5◇. If partner does not have the ♠Q, the small slam will be too risky unless partner has extra spade length.

Deal 13

1. No, you can't bid Blackwood. You don't even know what suit to play in! If you have a good fit with partner slam may be possible, but it is much too soon to worry about that.

2. Bid 5♦. You have three keycards, and this bid shows zero or three keycards.
3. Partner can bid 5♡ to ask for the ♦Q. Since this bid commits your side to at least 6♦, partner must be looking for a grand slam.
4. Bid 6♦. You do not have the ♦Q so you sign off with the lowest available diamond bid, in this case 6♦.

Deal 14

1. It's possible that you can make a grand slam. If partner has the top two heart honors with his seven-card heart suit you can count a sure thirteen tricks. You can find out what you need to know by bidding Roman Keycard Blackwood.
2. Bid 6♡. Partner is showing one key card which must be the ace or king of hearts. This is enough for slam but not enough for the grand slam.

Deal 15

1. Bid 2♡. With only three-card spade support you should show your own heart suit before raising partner.
2. 4NT will be Roman Keycard Blackwood in spades. When you jump to 4NT and a suit has not been bid and raised, the last suit bid (in this case spades) is the key suit.
3. 5♦ shows 0 or 3 keycards. You have only two keycards so partner could have three. Can partner have zero? No. If partner has no keycards then partner's spade suit is at best J107654. This would hardly be a good six-card suit. Partner must have three key cards.

Deal 16

1. Bid 3♦. This hand has three losers. You want to be in game, and if you bid only 2♦ partner might pass. You could ignore your diamonds and just rebid hearts. However, if you do this, you should rebid 4♡ not 3♡ since 3♡ is not forcing and you will be very unhappy if partner passes you there.
2. a) Partner is showing a preference for hearts. He likes hearts better than diamonds. This does not necessarily show a very good hand.
   b) You still have some slam chances. All partner needs is two of the three cards you are looking for: the ♠A, ♡K and ♦A.

c) Cuebid 4♣. After that it is up to partner. If partner does not cuebid or bid Blackwood then you may be off two or three keycards so you won't be able to go to slam. You cannot bid Roman Keycard Blackwood with a void. You won't know if partner has the wasted ♣A or another more useful keycard.

Deal 17

1. Bid 3♡. This bid simply tells partner that you have at least three hearts and like hearts better than diamonds.
2. Bid 5♡. This shows two keycards, in this case the ♡K and the ♣A, and tells partner that you do not have the ♡Q.
3. Bid 6◇ — one king. Yes, we know that you have two kings but you do not count the ♡K, since you have already showed that.

Deal 18

1. a) The key suit is spades. No trump suit had been specifically agreed up to this point. When partner bids Blackwood now, the last suit bid, in this case spades, is assumed to be the trump suit.
   b) Bid 5◇. You have three keycards, the ♠A, ♠K and ◇A. This response shows zero or three.
   c) Partner bids 5♡ to ask for the trump queen. Partner bids the next suit up skipping the trump suit if necessary. In this case the next suit up is hearts.

Deal 19

1. Bid 2♣. You have enough to force to game and you are likely to play the hand in spades. However, you cannot bid Jacoby 2NT with only three trumps and you are much to good for 4♠, which is preemptive. Bid 2♣ and see what partner does. You will support spades later.
2. Bid 4♠. If partner has a minimum you do not expect to make slam. Bid the spade game.
3. Bid 4NT, Roman Keycard Blackwood. Partner is showing a good six-card suit and 16-18 points. You have fifteen dummy points. If your side is not missing too many keycards, you should have excellent slam chances.

Deal 20

1. Partner is showing three keycards. His 5◊ bid shows zero or three keycards. In this auction partner must have three since he has shown a hand with 16+ points.

2. Bid 5♠ to ask for the trump queen. You ask for the trump queen by bidding the next step up, skipping the trump suit. Here 5♡ is the next step but since it is the trump suit you skip it and bid 5♠.

3. Bid 7♡. Partner is showing the ♡Q and the ♣K. You can count thirteen tricks — five hearts, six diamonds, two clubs and one spade — enough for the grand slam.

Deal 21

1. Bid 5♡. This shows two keycards without the spade queen. Your keycards are the ♡A and the ◊A.

2. Bid 6◊. This shows one king outside the trump suit. You have the ♣K.

Deal 22

1. No. Bid 4♣, Gerber to ask for aces. Gerber is used directly over notrump, not Blackwood. Here 4NT would be natural and invitational in notrump.

2. Bid 6NT. If partner shows two aces you expect to make small slam.

3. Partner bids 4♠ to show two aces.

Deal 23

1. Bid 4NT, Roman Keycard Blackwood. This great hand has only three possible losers, the three aces in the side suits. This is the only information you need to decide what contract to play in: 5◊, 6◊ or 7◊.

2. If partner has only one ace, partner will bid 5♣ and you can bid 5◊ for play. If partner has two or three aces, you want to be in slam, either a small slam or a grand slam. The only problem will occur if partner has no aces at all. In that case even the five-level is too high (unless partner has a void, which would probably be in clubs.) It's worth taking a chance.

Deal 24

1. Bid 5♣. You have one keycard, the ♡K, and 5♣ promises one or four keycards.

2. Diamonds are trumps, so 5♡ asks for the queen of diamonds. Respond with 5NT. This shows the ◇Q and a higher ranking king (the ♡K). Hearts are higher in rank than diamonds, the agreed trump suit, so bidding 6♡ will be going too high; thus 5NT.

Deal 25

1. Bid 4♡ and then 4NT. The first step is to set the trump suit. You do this by using Texas Transfer, which sets the trump suit as spades. Now you can bid Roman Keycard Blackwood with spades as the trump suit.

2. This auction asks partner to bid a slam if he has extra values. Partner can pick a spade slam if he has three or more spades or a notrump slam if he has only two spades. It shows a hand with five spades which is invitational to slam. This auction is similar to the auction

North	South
	2NT
3♡	3♠
3NT	

Here South is being asked to choose between 4♠ and 3NT.

Deal 26

1. You need two of the ♡K, the ♠A and the ♣K. You do not have diamond losers because you can trump diamonds in partner's hand.

2. Partner's 6◇ shows one king outside the trump suit. Since partner has splintered you know that partner does not have the ◇K (assuming you play splinters as we recommend). This means that partner must have the ♣K. Bid 7♡. Partner has already shown the ♡K and the ♠A. You know that you have two spade tricks, five heart tricks, one diamond and a diamond ruff in partner's hand and four club tricks for thirteen tricks.

Deal 27

1. Bid 2♠. You cannot bid Jacoby 2NT without four trumps. It is also acceptable to bid 1♠ since this bid is completely forcing (for one round).

2. Even though partner is showing no extra values you have great slam prospects. This hand is worth twenty-one dummy points in hearts. Once partner opens 1♡ you expect to have a good shot at slam.

3. If partner shows two keycards, grand slam is possible. Bid 5NT and ask for kings.

Deal 28

1. You plan to jump to 3◊ after partner bids a new suit. This will show partner that you have a hand worth about sixteen to eighteen points and an excellent six-card diamond suit.

2. Bid 5♣, showing four keycards for diamonds. It doesn't matter if you have already cuebid the ♡A, you still show it when partner asks you how many keycards you have. It would be too confusing to subtract keycards you have already shown in other ways.

Deal 29

1. Although you have a lot of high cards in clubs, you still have a hand worth twenty-two dummy points. This hand is so good that you want to be in slam anyway.

2. If partner bids 5♣ then partner has one of the three missing keycards, since 5♣ shows one or four keycards. If partner bids 5◊ then he has three keycards. (Since partner has opened the bidding it is extremely unlikely that he has zero. All of the remaining high cards only add up to ten points.)

Deal 30

1. Open 2♣: this hand is too good to open 1♠. You can make game in a major in your own hand and you have twenty-two HCP. Your plan is first to bid spades and then hearts and ask partner to pick which suit he likes better.

2. Once partner supports spades, the only cards needed for a grand slam are the ♠K and the ♣A. Blackwood is not recommended with a void. Unless partner has all the keycards you won't be able to tell whether partner has the useless ◊A or a more useful keycard.

3. Cuebid diamonds and show partner your first-round diamond control. See what partner has to say.

Deal 31

1. You need either the ◇A or ♣K to make a small slam. Even if partner has neither of these cards you might be able to make a small slam if partner has an entry in hearts and either the ♠Q to provide a discard for the ♣10 or the ♣Q and ♣J which will allow you to finesse in clubs. To make a grand slam you will need the ◇A and either the ♣K, the ◇K or the ♠Q.
2. If partner shows one keycard, bid 5NT. If partner has a king too, you can make a grand slam.

Deal 32

1. Pass. You do have an excellent hand but partner has made a pre-emptive bid. 1♡-4♡ shows 6-9 points and 5 trumps. You do not have enough to try for slam opposite partner's weak hand.
2. Hearts is the keysuit. When a trump suit has not been chosen (by being bid and raised) and you jump to 4NT Roman Keycard Blackwood the last suit bid is assumed to be the trump suit, in this case hearts. You should respond 5◇ showing 0 or 3 keycards.

Deal 33

1. Partner's bid shows a hand worth about twenty dummy points in support of spades. You have only promised six points so far, yet partner wants to play in game anyway. Partner has four spades but no singleton or void (since partner did not splinter). Since you have sixteen high card points you expect to make slam if you are not off two keycards.
2. Partner is showing both of the missing keycards. Bid 5NT; you may make a grand slam if partner has enough kings.

Deal 34

1. Bid 4◇. This is a splinter. It shows a singleton or void in diamonds, four-card support for clubs and a hand worth enough to make game (or about nineteen or more dummy points). The bid perfectly describes this hand, and partner can now decide how to proceed. If partner has a good fit or extra high cards you should have an excellent chance for slam. If partner has wasted diamond cards he will sign off in 5♣ unless he has a lot of extra values.

2. Yes. This excellent hand has very few losers. If partner wants to be in slam, so do you. If partner is missing no more than one of the club honors and the red aces, you should be able to make a small slam.

Deal 35

1. You plan is to show both of your black suits and see which one partner likes better. After that, you want to play in slam if partner has enough keycards. You will use Roman Keycard Blackwood to find out.
2. The 3♠ bid means that partner prefers spades to clubs. Partner has three or more spades. Spades has now been set as the trump suit, so 4NT now is Roman Keycard Blackwood.

Deal 36

1 a) Bid 4NT (Roman Keycard). Partner is showing four card spade support and about twenty dummy points (he jumped to game when you could have as few as six points). You have sixteen dummy points. Slam should be there. Check for key-cards.

   b) Bid 4NT (Roman Keycard). Partner has a distributional hand which is the equivalent of about twenty dummy points. His club shortness has not made your hand worse since you do not have a lot of wasted club cards. Slam should be there if you are not off too many keycards.

2. Partner's 5♣ bid shows 1 or 4 keycards. Since you have two partner cannot have four, so he must have one. You are missing two keycards and sadly you will have to sign off in 5♠.

Deal 37

1 a) Partner is showing four keycards (remember partner has shown a very strong hand). There are no keycards missing. Bid 5◊ to check for the trump queen. You may have a grand slam.

   b) Partner is showing three keycards. Bid 6♡.

2. The 6♡ bid shows the ♡Q without any side kings. A 5NT response shows the ♡Q and the ♠K (the only king which is higher-ranking than hearts).

Deal 38

1. Bid 3◊. A jump shift shows partner that you have a very big hand (19+ points) and suggests the possibility of slam. With 20 high card points this hand certainly qualifies.
2. Here 4NT is Roman Keycard Blackwood for hearts. When you jump to Blackwood over a naturally bid suit, it agrees this suit as trumps by inference. Since partner has just rebid his heart suit, a jump to 4NT agrees that suit.

Deal 39

1. Bid 4♠. Partner is showing ten to twelve dummy points. You have sixteen high card points enough for game opposite a limit raise.
2. Yes, this is Roman Keycard Blackwood with spades as the key suit. Respond 5◊ to show your three keycards.

Deal 40

1. Yes, 4NT is Roman Keycard Blackwood agreeing diamonds as trumps.
2. Bid 5♣ showing one keycard, the ◊K. We know that you do not have much but this is what partner is expecting. Answer his question.

SAMPLE AUCTIONS 5

Deal 1 - Dealer South

NORTH
♠ A K 2
♡ A 4
◇ K 2
♣ A J 10 9 8 7

☐

SOUTH
♠ 6 3
♡ K J 10 3 2
◇ A 9 5
♣ K Q 2

NORTH	SOUTH
	1♡
3♣	4♣
4NT	5♠
5NT	6◇
7♣	

Deal 2 - Dealer North

NORTH
♠ K Q J 10 3 2
♡ K Q 9
◇ A 2
♣ K J

☐

SOUTH
♠ A 9 5 4
♡ 8
◇ K Q 5
♣ 10 9 5 4 2

NORTH	SOUTH
1♠	3♠[1]
4NT	5♣
5♠	

1. Limit raise

Deal 3 - Dealer South

NORTH
♠ K Q 3
♡ A Q 2
◇ 7 5
♣ K Q 10 9 2

☐

SOUTH
♠ 6
♡ K J 9 4 3
◇ A 9 8 2
♣ A J 3

NORTH	SOUTH
	1♡
2♣	2◇
3♡ 1	4♣
4NT	5◇
6♡	

1. Forcing

Deal 4 - Dealer South

NORTH
♠ A Q 10 9 8 7 6
♡ 3
◇ A Q 5 4
♣ 2

☐

SOUTH
♠ J 2
♡ A Q 7 4
◇ K J 9 8
♣ A J 3

NORTH	SOUTH
	1NT
4♡ 1	4♠
4NT	5♡
6♠	

1. Texas Transfer

Deal 5 - Dealer North

NORTH
♠ A Q J 8 4 3 2
♡ 2
◇ 5
♣ A K Q 8

☐

SOUTH
♠ K 9 7 5
♡ A 7 3 2
◇ A J 3
♣ 5 4

NORTH	SOUTH
1♠	2NT
4NT	5◇
7♠	

Deal 6 - Dealer North

NORTH
♠ A J 5
♡ A Q 8 2
♢ K 2
♣ Q J 10 9

☐

SOUTH
♠ K Q 4 3 2
♡ K J 9 7 2
♢ A Q
♣ 2

NORTH	SOUTH
1NT	2♡
2♠	3♡
4♡	4NT
5♠	6♡

Deal 7 - Dealer South

NORTH
♠ A 5 3 2
♡ K Q 6 2
♢ 3
♣ Q 4 3 2

☐

SOUTH
♠ K Q 10 7 6
♡ A J 9 2
♢ 9 8
♣ A K

NORTH	SOUTH
	1♠
4♢[1]	4NT
5♣	6♠

1. Splinter

Deal 8 - Dealer North

NORTH
♠ K Q 10 5 4 2
♡ 5 4
♢ K 3 2
♣ 10 4

☐

SOUTH
♠ J 9 3
♡ A
♢ A Q 5 4
♣ A K 9 8 5

NORTH	SOUTH
2♠	2NT
3♢[1]	4NT
5♣	5♢
6♢	6♠

1. Diamond feature

Deal 9 - Dealer North

NORTH
♠ K Q
♡ A Q J
◇ A Q J 10 8 7 5
♣ A

☐

SOUTH
♠ A 2
♡ 10 5 4 3
◇ K 9 2
♣ Q 9 8 7

NORTH	SOUTH
2♣	2◇
3◇	4◇
4NT	5♡
5NT	6♣
6◇	

Deal 10 - Dealer South

NORTH
♠ A 6
♡ A K Q 10 9 8 7
◇ A Q 8
♣ 7

☐

SOUTH
♠ K 10 4 3 2
♡ J 6 3
◇ K 9
♣ A K 2

NORTH	SOUTH
	1♠
2♡	3♡
4NT	5♣
5NT	6♠
7♡ or 7NT	

Deal 11 - Dealer North

NORTH
♠ K J 2
♡ K Q 10
◇ A J 9 8
♣ K 10 2

☐

SOUTH
♠ Q 10 9
♡ A 9 8
◇ K Q 3
♣ A Q 6 4

NORTH	SOUTH
1NT	4♣[1]
4♡	6NT

1. Gerber

Deal 12 - Dealer South

NORTH
♠ K 8 4 3
♡ A J 4 3
◇ A J 3
♣ K 9 8

[ ]

SOUTH
♠ A Q 10 9 7
♡ K 5
◇ K Q 10 3 2
♣ 3

NORTH	SOUTH
	1♠
2NT	4◇
4NT	5♣
5◇	6◇
6♠	

Deal 13 - Dealer North

NORTH
♠ K 9 8 7 3
♡ 9
◇ A K 6 5 4 3
♣ A

[ ]

SOUTH
♠ A Q
♡ A J 10 8
◇ Q J 2
♣ Q 4 3 2

NORTH	SOUTH
1◇	1♡
1♠	2♣¹
2♠	3◇
4♣	4♡
4♠²	4NT
5◇	5NT
6◇	7◇

1. Fourth suit — game force
2. Second round control

Deal 14 - Dealer North

NORTH
♠ 9
♡ K J 10 9 8 7 4
◇ 6 2
♣ J 9 5

[ ]

SOUTH
♠ A K 5 4
♡ Q 5 3
◇ A K Q 3
♣ A 2

NORTH	SOUTH
3♡	4NT
5♣	6♡

Deal 15 - Dealer South

NORTH
♠ Q 9 8
♡ A Q J 4 2
♢ K 6
♣ A 5 3

☐

SOUTH
♠ A K J 4 3 2
♡ K 3
♢ Q 10 4
♣ K Q

NORTH	SOUTH
	1♠
2♡	3♠
4NT	5♡
6♠	

Deal 16 - Dealer North

NORTH
♠ 5
♡ A Q J 10 9 5 4
♢ K Q J 9 5
♣ —

☐

SOUTH
♠ K 8 4 3 2
♡ K 6 2
♢ 10 8
♣ A Q 3

NORTH	SOUTH
1♡	1♠
3♢	3♡
4♣	4♡

Deal 17 - Dealer South

NORTH
♠ A J
♡ A Q J 7 2
♢ K J 9 8 7
♣ 8

☐

SOUTH
♠ K Q 9 8
♡ K 6 5 4
♢ Q 10
♣ A J 7

NORTH	SOUTH
	1NT
2♢	2♡
3♢	3♡
4NT	5♡
6♡	

Deal 18 - Dealer South

NORTH
♠ 5 4
♡ A K 7 6 2
◇ K Q
♣ K Q J 10

☐

SOUTH
♠ A K Q 9 8 7 6
♡ 3
◇ A 7 2
♣ 5 4

NORTH	SOUTH
	1♠
2♡	3♠
4NT	5◇
5♡	6♠

Deal 19 - Dealer North

NORTH
♠ A Q 5 4 3
♡ K 9 8
◇ Q 7 2
♣ Q 3

☐

SOUTH
♠ K 9 8
♡ A 4 3
◇ K 3
♣ A 10 9 8 7

NORTH	SOUTH
1♠	2♣
2NT	4♠

Deal 20 - Dealer South

NORTH
♠ 3
♡ J 10 8 7
◇ A K Q J 9 8
♣ A 2

☐

SOUTH
♠ A 5
♡ A K Q 5 4
◇ 5 4
♣ K 8 4 3

NORTH	SOUTH
	1♡
2NT	3♡
4NT	5◇
5♠	6♣
7♡	

Deal 21 - Dealer South

NORTH
♠ A K Q 5 4
♡ K Q 6 4
◇ K J 2
♣ 3

□

SOUTH
♠ 9 8 7 6
♡ A 9 8
◇ A 5
♣ K Q 9 5

NORTH	SOUTH
	1♣
1♠	2♠
4NT	5♡
6♠	

Deal 22 - Dealer South

NORTH
♠ K 8 4
♡ A Q
◇ K Q 10
♣ K 9 8 7 5

□

SOUTH
♠ Q J 9
♡ K J 5
◇ A J 9 3
♣ Q J 10

NORTH	SOUTH
	1NT
4♣[1]	4♡
4NT[2]	Pass

1. Gerber
2. To play

Deal 23 - Dealer South

NORTH
♠ 5
♡ 5
◇ A K Q 9 8 7
♣ K Q J 10 9

□

SOUTH
♠ A J 7
♡ Q 10 8 7 2
◇ J 10 3 2
♣ A 2

NORTH	SOUTH
	1♡
2◇	3◇
4NT	5♡
6◇	

Deal 24 - Dealer North

NORTH
♠ —
♡ K Q 10 9 7
◇ Q J 7 3 2
♣ Q 9 5

□

SOUTH
♠ A J
♡ J 8 6
◇ K 8 4
♣ A K J 10 6

NORTH	SOUTH
1♡	2♣
2◇	3♡
4♡	4NT
5♣	5◇
6♡	

Deal 25 - Dealer South

NORTH
♠ K Q 10 9 6 2
♡ 9
◇ K 7
♣ A J 8 5

□

SOUTH
♠ A J
♡ K J 8 4
◇ A Q 5 4
♣ K Q 10

NORTH	SOUTH
	2NT
4♡	4♠
4NT	5♡
6♠	

Deal 26 - Dealer North

NORTH
♠ K
♡ A Q 8 6 3
◇ A 10 6
♣ A Q J 10

□

SOUTH
♠ A Q 10
♡ K 10 9 8 7 2
◇ J
♣ K 8 5

NORTH	SOUTH
1♡	4◇¹
4NT	5♡
5NT	6◇
7♡	

1. Splinter

Deal 27 - Dealer South

NORTH
♠ A Q 10 9 8 6
♡ A Q 8
◇ A 7
♣ K 2

SOUTH
♠ K 2
♡ K J 9 4 3 2
◇ K 4
♣ Q J 6

NORTH	SOUTH
	1♡
2♠	3♡
4NT	5♣
6♡	

Deal 28 - Dealer North

NORTH
♠ 8
♡ A 10 5
◇ A K J 10 8 7
♣ A J 2

SOUTH
♠ A 9 5 4 3
♡ K Q J 3
◇ Q 3 2
♣ K

NORTH	SOUTH
1◇	1♠
3◇	4NT
5♣	7◇ (or 7NT)

Deal 29 - Dealer North

NORTH
♠ K Q J
♡ K J 6 5 2
◇ Q J 10 5
♣ 5

SOUTH
♠ 3
♡ A Q 10 9 3
◇ K 9 8
♣ A K Q J

NORTH	SOUTH
1♡	2NT
3♣	4NT
5♣	5♡

Deal 30 - Dealer South

NORTH
♠ K 9 3
♡ 10 4
◇ A Q J 2
♣ 9 8 7 2

☐

SOUTH
♠ A Q J 10 5
♡ A K Q 7 5
◇ —
♣ K Q J

NORTH	SOUTH
	2♣
2◇	2♠
3♠	4◇
5◇	6♠

Deal 31 - Dealer South

NORTH
♠ 9 8 5 4
♡ 6 3 2
◇ A K 7
♣ 8 4 2

☐

SOUTH
♠ A K
♡ A K Q J 10 8 7 5
◇ 9
♣ A 10

NORTH	SOUTH
	2♣
2◇	2♡
3♡	4NT
5♣	5NT
6◇	7NT

Deal 32 - Dealer North

NORTH
♠ K 9 3
♡ A K 8 3 2
◇ K Q 9
♣ A 5

☐

SOUTH
♠ J 4
♡ Q J 10 9 5 4
◇ 5
♣ K 10 8 3

NORTH	SOUTH
1♡	4♡

Deal 33 - Dealer North

NORTH
♠ A J 7 6
♡ K J 10 7
♢ K 5
♣ K Q J

SOUTH
♠ Q 9 5 4
♡ A Q 8
♢ A 7
♣ A 5 3 2

NORTH	SOUTH
1♣	1♠
4♠	4NT
5♣	6♠

Deal 34 - Dealer South

NORTH
♠ 7
♡ A 2
♢ Q 5 3
♣ K Q J 10 8 7 6

SOUTH
♠ A K 3
♡ K Q J 8 5
♢ 9
♣ A 5 4 2

NORTH	SOUTH
	1♡
2♣	4♢[1]
4NT	5♡
6♣	

1. Splinter

Deal 35 - Dealer North

NORTH
♠ A 9
♡ A K 3
♢ A 9 6 5
♣ Q 6 4 2

SOUTH
♠ K Q J 10 7
♡ 5
♢ K 10
♣ A K J 9 8

NORTH	SOUTH
1NT	2♡[1]
2♠	3♣
4♣	4NT
5♢	5♡
5NT	7♣

1. Transfer

Deal 36 - Dealer South

NORTH
♠ Q 10 9 8 2
♡ A 5 4
◇ K 10
♣ A J 3

☐

SOUTH
♠ K J 7 6
♡ K Q J
◇ A Q J 8 7
♣ 2

NORTH	SOUTH
	1◇
1♠	4♣¹
4NT	5♡
6♠	

1. Splinter

Deal 37 - Dealer South

NORTH
♠ A 4
♡ 7 5 4 2
◇ K Q J 7 5
♣ K 2

☐

SOUTH
♠ 2
♡ A K Q J 10 8
◇ A Q J 9
♣ A J

NORTH	SOUTH
	2♣
2◇	2♡
4NT	5♣
5◇	6♡
7♡	

Deal 38 - Dealer North

NORTH
♠ 10 7 5
♡ A K Q 9 8 7
◇ 7 2
♣ A 4

☐

SOUTH
♠ K Q
♡ J 10
◇ A K Q 10 3
♣ K Q 5 3

NORTH	SOUTH
1♡	3◇
3♡	4NT
5◇	6♡

Deal 39 - Dealer South

NORTH
♠ A Q 8 4
♡ K 10 5 4
◇ 10 9 3
♣ 9 4

☐

SOUTH
♠ K 10 7 6 5
♡ A 6
◇ A J 8 6
♣ K J

NORTH	SOUTH
	1♠
3♠	4♠

Deal 40 - Dealer North

NORTH
♠ 7 6
♡ 9
◇ K Q 10 9 6 5 4
♣ 9 8 4

☐

SOUTH
♠ A Q 5 2
♡ A K 5
◇ J 7 3
♣ A K Q

NORTH	SOUTH
3◇	4NT
5♣	6◇

section

PRACTICE HANDS

Hand 1 - Dealer South

♠ A K 2
♡ A 4
◇ K 2
♣ A J 10 9 8 7

YOUR AUCTION

NORTH	SOUTH

Hand 2 - Dealer North

♠ K Q J 10 3 2
♡ K Q 9
◇ A 2
♣ K J

YOUR AUCTION

NORTH	SOUTH

Hand 3 - Dealer South

♠ K Q 3
♡ A Q 2
◇ 7 5
♣ K Q 10 9 2

YOUR AUCTION

NORTH	SOUTH

Hand 4 - Dealer South

♠ A Q 10 9 8 7 6
♡ 3
◇ A Q 5 4
♣ 2

YOUR AUCTION

NORTH	SOUTH

Hand 5 - Dealer North

♠ A Q J 8 4 3 2
♡ 2
◇ 5
♣ A K Q 8

YOUR AUCTION

NORTH	SOUTH

Hand 6 - Dealer North

♠ A J 5
♡ A Q 8 2
◇ K 2
♣ Q J 10 9

YOUR AUCTION

NORTH   SOUTH

Hand 7 - Dealer South

♠ A 5 3 2
♡ K Q 6 2
◇ 3
♣ Q 4 3 2

YOUR AUCTION

NORTH   SOUTH

Hand 8 - Dealer North

♠ K Q 10 5 4 2
♡ 5 4
◇ K 3 2
♣ 10 4

YOUR AUCTION

NORTH   SOUTH

Hand 9 - Dealer North

♠ K Q
♡ A Q J
◇ A Q J 10 8 7 5
♣ A

YOUR AUCTION

NORTH   SOUTH

Hand 10 - Dealer South

♠ A 6
♡ A K Q 10 9 8 7
◇ A Q 8
♣ 7

YOUR AUCTION

NORTH   SOUTH

Hand 11 - Dealer North

♠ K J 2
♡ K Q 10
◇ A J 9 8
♣ K 10 2

YOUR AUCTION

NORTH	SOUTH

Hand 12 - Dealer South

♠ K 8 4 3
♡ A J 4 3
◇ A J 3
♣ K 9 8

YOUR AUCTION

NORTH	SOUTH

Hand 13 - Dealer North

♠ K 9 8 7 3
♡ 9
◇ A K 6 5 4 3
♣ A

YOUR AUCTION

NORTH	SOUTH

Hand 14 - Dealer North

♠ 9
♡ K J 10 9 8 7 4
◇ 6 2
♣ J 9 5

YOUR AUCTION

NORTH	SOUTH

Hand 15 - Dealer South

♠ Q 9 8
♡ A Q J 4 2
◇ K 6
♣ A 5 3

YOUR AUCTION

NORTH	SOUTH

Hand 16 - Dealer North

♠ 5
♡ A Q J 10 9 5 4
◇ K Q J 9 5
♣ —

YOUR AUCTION

NORTH	SOUTH

Hand 17 - Dealer South

♠ A J
♡ A Q J 7 2
◇ K J 9 8 7
♣ 8

YOUR AUCTION

NORTH	SOUTH

Hand 18 - Dealer North

♠ 5 4
♡ A K 7 6 2
◇ K Q
♣ K Q J 10

YOUR AUCTION

NORTH	SOUTH

Hand 19 - Dealer North

♠ A Q 5 4 3
♡ K 9 8
◇ Q 7 2
♣ Q 3

YOUR AUCTION

NORTH	SOUTH

Hand 20 - Dealer South

♠ 3
♡ J 10 8 7
◇ A K Q J 9 8
♣ A 2

YOUR AUCTION

NORTH	SOUTH

Hand 21 - Dealer North

♠ A K Q 5 4
♡ K Q 6 4
◇ K J 2
♣ 3

YOUR AUCTION	
NORTH	SOUTH

Hand 22 - Dealer South

♠ K 8 4
♡ A Q
◇ K Q 10
♣ K 9 8 7 5

YOUR AUCTION	
NORTH	SOUTH

Hand 23 - Dealer South

♠ 5
♡ 5
◇ A K Q 9 8 7
♣ K Q J 10 9

YOUR AUCTION	
NORTH	SOUTH

Hand 24 - Dealer North

♠ —
♡ K Q 10 9 7
◇ Q J 7 3 2
♣ Q 9 5

YOUR AUCTION	
NORTH	SOUTH

Hand 25 - Dealer South

♠ K Q 10 9 6 2
♡ 9
◇ K 7
♣ A J 8 5

YOUR AUCTION	
NORTH	SOUTH

Hand 26 - Dealer North

♠ K
♡ A Q 8 6 3
◇ A 10 6
♣ A Q J 10

YOUR AUCTION	
NORTH	SOUTH

Hand 27 - Dealer South

♠ A Q 10 9 8 6
♡ A Q 8
◇ A 7
♣ K 2

YOUR AUCTION	
NORTH	SOUTH

Hand 28 - Dealer North

♠ 8
♡ A 10 5
◇ A K J 10 8 7
♣ A J 2

YOUR AUCTION	
NORTH	SOUTH

Hand 29 - Dealer South

♠ K Q J
♡ K J 6 5 2
◇ Q J 10 5
♣ 5

YOUR AUCTION	
NORTH	SOUTH

Hand 30 - Dealer South

♠ K 9 3
♡ 10 4
◇ A Q J 2
♣ 9 8 7 2

YOUR AUCTION	
NORTH	SOUTH

Hand 31 - Dealer South

♠ 9 8 5 4
♡ 6 3 2
◇ A K 7
♣ 8 4 2

YOUR AUCTION	
NORTH	SOUTH

Hand 32 - Dealer North

♠ K 9 3
♡ A K 8 3 2
◇ K Q 9
♣ A 5

YOUR AUCTION	
NORTH	SOUTH

Hand 33 - Dealer North

♠ A J 7 6
♡ K J 10 7
◇ K 5
♣ K Q J

YOUR AUCTION	
NORTH	SOUTH

Hand 34 - Dealer South

♠ 7
♡ A 2
◇ Q 5 3
♣ K Q J 10 8 7 6

YOUR AUCTION	
NORTH	SOUTH

Hand 35 - Dealer North

♠ A 9
♡ A K 3
◇ A 9 6 5
♣ Q 6 4 2

YOUR AUCTION	
NORTH	SOUTH

Hand 36 - Dealer South

♠ Q 10 9 8 2
♡ A 5 4
◇ K 10
♣ A J 3

YOUR AUCTION	
NORTH	SOUTH

Hand 37 - Dealer South

♠ A 4
♡ 7 5 4 2
◇ K Q J 7 5
♣ K 2

YOUR AUCTION	
NORTH	SOUTH

Hand 38 - Dealer North

♠ 10 7 5
♡ A K Q 9 8 7
◇ 7 2
♣ K 2

YOUR AUCTION	
NORTH	SOUTH

Hand 39 - Dealer South

♠ A Q 8 4
♡ K 10 5 4
◇ 10 9 3
♣ 9 4

YOUR AUCTION	
NORTH	SOUTH

Hand 40 - Dealer North

♠ 7 6
♡ 9
◇ K Q 10 9 6 5 4
♣ 9 8 4

YOUR AUCTION	
NORTH	SOUTH

Hand 1 - Dealer South

♠ 6 3
♡ K J 10 3 2
◇ A 9 5
♣ K Q 2

YOUR AUCTION

NORTH   SOUTH

Hand 2 - Dealer North

♠ A 9 5 4
♡ 8
◇ K Q 5
♣ 10 9 5 4

YOUR AUCTION

NORTH   SOUTH

Hand 3 - Dealer South

♠ 6
♡ K J 9 4 3
◇ A 9 8 2
♣ A J 3

YOUR AUCTION

NORTH   SOUTH

Hand 4 - Dealer South

♠ J 2
♡ A Q J 4
◇ K J 9 8
♣ A J 3

YOUR AUCTION

NORTH   SOUTH

Hand 5 - Dealer North

♠ K 9 7 5
♡ A 7 3 2
◇ A J 3
♣ 5 4

YOUR AUCTION

NORTH   SOUTH

Hand 6 - Dealer North

♠ K Q 4 3 2
♡ K J 9 7 2
◇ A 2
♣ 2

YOUR AUCTION

NORTH	SOUTH

Hand 7 - Dealer South

♠ K Q 10 7 6
♡ A J 9 2
◇ 9 8
♣ A K

YOUR AUCTION

NORTH	SOUTH

Hand 8 - Dealer North

♠ J 9 3
♡ A
◇ A Q 5 4
♣ A K 9 8 5

YOUR AUCTION

NORTH	SOUTH

Hand 9 - Dealer North

♠ A 2
♡ 10 5 4 3
◇ K 9 2
♣ Q 9 8 7

YOUR AUCTION

NORTH	SOUTH

Hand 10 - Dealer South

♠ K 10 4 3 2
♡ J 6 3
◇ K 9
♣ A K 2

YOUR AUCTION

NORTH	SOUTH

Hand 11 - Dealer North

♠ Q 10 9
♡ A 9 8
◇ K Q 3
♣ A Q 6 4

YOUR AUCTION

NORTH	SOUTH

Hand 12 - Dealer South

♠ A Q 10 9 7
♡ K 5
◇ K Q 10 3 2
♣ 3

YOUR AUCTION

NORTH	SOUTH

Hand 13 - Dealer North

♠ A Q
♡ A J 10 8
◇ Q J 2
♣ Q 4 3 2

YOUR AUCTION

NORTH	SOUTH

Hand 14 - Dealer North

♠ A K 5 4
♡ Q 5 3
◇ A K Q 3
♣ A 2

YOUR AUCTION

NORTH	SOUTH

Hand 15 - Dealer South

♠ A K J 4 3 2
♡ K 3
◇ Q 10 4
♣ K Q

YOUR AUCTION

NORTH	SOUTH

Hand 16 - Dealer North

♠ K 8 4 3 2
♡ K 6 2
◇ 9 8
♣ A Q 3

YOUR AUCTION
NORTH   SOUTH

Hand 17 - Dealer South

♠ K Q 9 8
♡ K 6 5 4
◇ Q 10
♣ A J 7

YOUR AUCTION
NORTH   SOUTH

Hand 18 - Dealer North

♠ A K Q 9 8 7 6
♡ 3
◇ A 7 2
♣ 5 4

YOUR AUCTION
NORTH   SOUTH

Hand 19 - Dealer North

♠ K 9 8
♡ A 4 3
◇ K 3
♣ A 10 9 8 7

YOUR AUCTION
NORTH   SOUTH

Hand 20 - Dealer South

♠ A 5
♡ A K Q 5 4
◇ 5 4
♣ K 8 4 3

YOUR AUCTION
NORTH   SOUTH

Hand 21 - Dealer North

♠ 9 8 7 6
♡ A 9 8
◇ A 5
♣ K Q 9 5

YOUR AUCTION

NORTH   SOUTH

Hand 22 - Dealer South

♠ Q J 9
♡ K J 5
◇ A J 9 3
♣ Q J 10

YOUR AUCTION

NORTH   SOUTH

Hand 23 - Dealer South

♠ A J 7
♡ Q 10 8 7 2
◇ J 10 3 2
♣ A 2

YOUR AUCTION

NORTH   SOUTH

Hand 24 - Dealer North

♠ A J
♡ J 8 6
◇ K 8 4
♣ A K J 10 6

YOUR AUCTION

NORTH   SOUTH

Hand 25 - Dealer South

♠ A J
♡ K J 8 4
◇ A Q 5 4
♣ K Q 10

YOUR AUCTION

NORTH   SOUTH

Hand 26 - Dealer North

♠ A Q 10
♡ K 10 9 8 7 2
◇ J
♣ K 8 5

YOUR AUCTION

NORTH	SOUTH

Hand 27 - Dealer South

♠ K 2
♡ K J 9 4 3 2
◇ K 4
♣ Q J 6

YOUR AUCTION

NORTH	SOUTH

Hand 28 - Dealer North

♠ A 9 5 4 3
♡ K Q J 3
◇ Q 3 2
♣ K

YOUR AUCTION

NORTH	SOUTH

Hand 29 - Dealer South

♠ 3
♡ A Q 10 9 3
◇ K 9 8
♣ A K Q J

YOUR AUCTION

NORTH	SOUTH

Hand 30 - Dealer South

♠ A Q J 10 5
♡ A K Q 7 5
◇ —
♣ K Q J

YOUR AUCTION

NORTH	SOUTH

Hand 31 - Dealer South

♠ A K
♡ AKQJ10875
◇ 9
♣ A 10

YOUR AUCTION

NORTH   SOUTH

Hand 32 - Dealer North

♠ J 4
♡ Q J 10 8 7 5
◇ 5
♣ K 10 8 3

YOUR AUCTION

NORTH   SOUTH

Hand 33 - Dealer North

♠ Q 9 5 4
♡ A Q 8
◇ A 7
♣ A 5 3 2

YOUR AUCTION

NORTH   SOUTH

Hand 34 - Dealer South

♠ A K 3
♡ K Q J 8 5
◇ 9
♣ A 5 4 2

YOUR AUCTION

NORTH   SOUTH

Hand 35 - Dealer North

♠ K Q J 10 7
♡ 5
◇ K 10
♣ A K J 9 8

YOUR AUCTION

NORTH   SOUTH

Hand 36 - Dealer South

♠ K J 7 6
♡ K Q J
♢ A Q J 8 7
♣ 2

YOUR AUCTION

NORTH	SOUTH

Hand 37 - Dealer South

♠ 2
♡ A K Q J 10 8
♢ A Q J 9
♣ A J

YOUR AUCTION

NORTH	SOUTH

Hand 38 - Dealer North

♠ K Q
♡ J 10
♢ A K Q 10 3
♣ K Q 5 3

YOUR AUCTION

NORTH	SOUTH

Hand 39 - Dealer South

♠ K 10 7 6 5
♡ A 6
♢ A J 8 6
♣ K J

YOUR AUCTION

NORTH	SOUTH

Hand 40 - Dealer North

♠ A Q 5 2
♡ A K 5
♢ J 7 3
♣ A K Q

YOUR AUCTION

NORTH	SOUTH